JOB INTERVIEW QUESTIONS

A Complete Guide to Discover All the Possible Questions of a Job Interview and to Give the Best Answers with Advanced Skills and Techniques

Brad James

Legal & Disclaimer

The information contained in this book and its contents is not designed to replace or take the place of any form of medical or professional advice; and is not meant to replace the need for independent medical, financial, legal or other professional advice or services, as may be required. The content and information in this book has been provided for educational and entertainment purposes only.

The content and information contained in this book has been compiled from sources deemed reliable, and it is accurate to the best of the Author's knowledge, information and belief. However, the Author cannot guarantee its accuracy and validity and cannot be held liable for any errors and/or omissions. Further, changes are periodically made to this book as and when needed. Where appropriate and/or necessary, you must consult a professional (including but not limited to your doctor, attorney, financial advisor or such other professional advisor) before using any of the suggested remedies, techniques, or information in this book.

Upon using the contents and information contained in this book, you agree to hold harmless the Author from and against any damages, costs, and expenses, including any legal fees potentially resulting from the application of any of the information provided by this book. This disclaimer applies to any loss, damages or injury caused by the use and application, whether directly or indirectly, of any advice or information presented, whether for breach of contract, tort, negligence, personal injury, criminal intent, or under any other cause of action.

You agree to accept all risks of using the information presented inside this book.

You agree that by continuing to read this book, where appropriate and/or necessary, you shall consult a professional (including but not limited to your doctor, attorney, or financial advisor or such needed) before using any of the suggested remedies, techniques, or information in this book.

4

Table of Content

INTRODUCTION

Advice the Best Answers: take inspiration from the questions you will find in this guide and practice as much as possible in front of the mirror, it will seem strange but it is the best technique to dissolve and become aware of what needs to be said.

Don't learn the answers by heart because this could be a problem if we are asked questions that we have not prepared ourselves, the important thing is to bring out our skills and competences and why these make you the best candidate, so make a list with key points to include in your answers.

Don't digress too much, try to understand what is asked of you and what the interviewer wants to hear and try to coincide and not talk about personal, family, sentimental or other problems.
The fact that you're reading this book suggests that the stakes are high. Perhaps you're anticipating an interview for your dream job or trying to get into a competitive school. In any case, you may

recognize that impressing an interviewer is the next crucial step in your career.

You'll be relieved to know that interviewing is an easy skill to master. You don't need physical strength or superior intellect. While interviewing hundreds of candidates over the years, I've seen interviews that fall into three categories. About 70% are disappointing. Unprepared candidates struggle through their interviews with answers that are either vague or don't address the questions I ask.

The most important thing to remember at the end of the day is that you should always be yourself. The people interviewing you want to know who you are and why they should pick you above everyone else! Don't stress yourself to the point that you overthink everything in the interview, but be prepared by reading through these questions, answers, and explanations.

Trying to **answer** interview questions correctly can be hard, but this book will allow you to explore the different techniques that will allow you to ace the interview. By the end of this, interviews will be a breeze!

By reading this book, you will not only get the best and professional advice to win an interview, but also how to finalize it and get your dream job.

CHAPTER 1: OPENING QUESTIONS

How would you define success?

This answer depends on your goals and ambition. How far do you see yourself? Undoubtedly success is the topmost step of a ladder but then it varies from person to person as in how many and what steps they consider. Try answering this more tactfully.

Answer: Success to me is when you do your job to your own satisfaction and you get a similar response from the employer as well. For me success is what makes me happy, and a job done well, a task performed excellently is the true definition of success professionally.

What did you do to prepare for this interview?

Answer: I started my morning making sure I got enough rest before heading here so I could be relaxed. I got ready, got dressed in what I picked out this morning, and had a nice breakfast. The night before I made sure to go over my resume once more and freshen up on what questions I might be asked. On the way here, I listened to some relaxing music to reduce stress so that I would be able to relax and give honest answers throughout!

What and where did you study?

Interviewers will definitely want to know more about your schooling and education, or any certificates or courses you might have taken rather than just work history at the moment. Start with your high school if you haven't graduated more than 15 years ago. Then, move onto college and any post-graduate education you have as well. State what you studied and the degrees that you received. Mention classes that you did well in, and don't forget about extra-curricular activities. Aside from just schooling, mention any outside classes you might have had, seminars attended, programs enrolled in, and certificates held. They want to know everything about the things that you have already been taught.

Answer: I started my educational career back in the Illinois suburbs, graduating in the top 10 percent of my class while also participating in soccer and student government. I then went on to study at DePaul University, getting my Bachelor's degree in Arts and Sciences. From there, I took an internship before heading back for my Master's degree.

Which three words best describe you?

Do your homework before coming to the interview so that you are able to jot down the best words that describe you in relevance to your job. You can answer this question with great ease only if you had prepared for this at home.

Answer: I would say I am a good team player with a nice, amicable attitude. I am very detail oriented and can attentively focus on minor details most accurately.

Can you tell me any three of your pet peeves?

The best way is to not let out your weaknesses yourself. Do not share your pet peeves even if you have any. Just work around a nice answer to handle this question. A sample answer is given below.

Answer: I do not have any particular pet peeves. When something bothers me, I analyze the situation and then take appropriate measures to set things straight.

What are your biggest Strengths?

This is the best time to present you as the worthiest candidate for the job. Assess what are the most wanted skills for the job and match them against your natural strengths. You can be an excellent motivating leader or a person with extra ordinary logical skills to overcome conflict situations.

Answer: My biggest strength would be my superb command on xxxx.

Tell me about your closest friend.

Whether you let people be close, are you friendly enough and often this question is succeeded by questions like how will your best friend describe you.

Answer: I am very close to two people, who are my dearest friends, Sarah and Michelle. The three of us have been together for more than eighteen years now and have seen many ups and downs of life. We now live in different cities but we make the effort to stay in touch with each other.

Where do you see yourself in next five to ten years?

This is a chance to highlight your bright future and to portray yourself in the way you want to. Give the right answer so that it leaves no other choice for the employer but to hire you. Read about the most successful people in your career and following their footsteps try to come up with your own objectives. Try to answer this intelligently and bag this job before you walk out of the room.

Answer: In the next five years, I see myself being the best sales person this company ever had. I can go to any length to make sure that I achieve my goals successfully within time. I will work to becoming the best in my field by getting all the knowledge and training that my job requires. I am totally prepared to take on any challenge that comes across in performing my responsibilities.

What is your favorite animal and why?

Make an intelligent choice of an animal that has the best set of characteristics to support your job requirements. For example, dolphin is intelligent and intuitive, lion is aggressive and dominating and elephant is strong and loyal.

Answer: My favorite animal is Elephant. I like him for his amazing strength and impressive loyalty, which you seldom find in animal kingdom.

Which activities take most of your free time?

The main idea behind asking this question is to know how healthy a life you have outside the professional one. If you lead a healthy life, then the positivity will certainly help you be friendly and nice to colleagues. It also gives more stability to your personality. Loners and party fanatics are not the best options for this question.

Answer: I love watching TV with family, do some fun cooking at weekends and I play tennis with friends too.

What are your biggest weaknesses?

This question does not require you to be utterly honest rather be a little tactful and share your harmless weakness that can be managed/ improved with ease. Your weakness should ideally not affect your quality of work.

Answer: Making sure that everybody around me understands things to the level that I do would be my biggest weakness. I am always looking to helping out others so that they can also perform excellently in a team.

Are you a persistent person? Describe an incident from your current/past job that supports this opinion.

Answer: In answer to your question, I am a persistent person. Let me give you a situation that demonstrates my use of persistence to complete a project.

Then you move on to the second part of the question and tell about what action you performed that demonstrates your persistence in a favorable light.

Tell me a little bit about yourself.

This, without a doubt, will be one of the first questions asked when it comes time for your interview. Even if there was a part of the application process that asked you this, you will still be likely to have to answer in person. They want to hear first and foremost about who you are. This is their opportunity to get to know you. Here, they want to get a sense of how you feel about yourself. Many positions will require confidence and self-assurance. You'll want to let them know that you are self-aware and that you believe in yourself and your own abilities.

Answer: To answer this, start off with what you believe is most important about yourself. Follow up with a brief history of your experiences, and then discuss why you are here at the interview and why you are looking to land this position. This may make for a short answer, but it is a good outline for what you will want your answer to be as well. Remember to recite your answer out loud or else it might end up sounding awkward when you really try to discuss who you are and your past achievements. This is an example of what you might say:

Can you describe a situation in your life that makes you prouder than anything else?

The person conducting the interview is asking this because they want to hear about your great accomplishments! This is the time for you to brag about yourself a little bit so that they can see that you are the one for the job. Make sure to choose an accomplishment that shows off your character or your relevance to the job. If you are incredibly proud of your massive shoe collection, that's great, but it's not going to make you look good in the interview.

Answer: I would have to say that I am proud of my dedication. It allowed me to go to school full-time while also working as a part-time intern to help advance my career a bit further. I'm proud of myself for putting in the hard work because it's certainly paid off so far!

What is a personal goal that you have in life?

Your interviewer can already guess that your goals revolve around your career, which is why you are trying to get a job at the moment. What you will want to focus on for this question is not just what your career goals are, but what you might be wanting in your personal life as well. Maybe you want to be a better person, someone that's more giving, a great father/mother, or start to live a healthier lifestyle. This question is non-work related, so share what your personal dreams are! This will help to show that you are focused on excellence and are dedicated to a purpose.

Answer: One of my personal goals is to eventually complete a triathlon. I have done various other races, but this is something that I have been working towards for several years. I am hopeful that one day I'll be able to not only finish one but to place in a top position as well!

What kinds of hobbies do you have, or what do you like to do in your free time?

The person conducting the interview is going to start getting more into what kind of things you like to do in your free time. they are curious about the personality traits you have, and what kind of commitment that you partake in. Never say that you don't have any hobbies, and don't let your hobbies be something like, hanging out with friends. Dig deep and find something that you enjoy that makes you happy. You might not consider it a hobby at the moment, but any little trade or craft you have can help them see that you are passionate, dedicated, and responsible. **Answer:** I would have to say that one of my hobbies includes cooking. I love trying out new foods and experimenting with recipes as often as possible. I also love gardening and have my own herb garden that I get to experiment with. It's a fun way for me to learn new things and also helps to keep me relaxed in my free time.

If I asked the people closest to you, how would they describe you?

Some people have no issue describing themselves, but it can be the perspective of others that can really help define who you are. The person conducting the interview is asking this question because they want to determine where you will fit in at this company. What roles do you play in your personal life, and what role will you play in this professional setting? Keep the description short, and base it on the best qualities that you might often hear from others.

Answer: I would think that my friends describe me as being funny and somewhat outgoing. I love making people laugh and am always looking for a way to turn a boring situation into a fun one, and I think those that are closest to me appreciate that. They would also say I am reliable because I never mind helping out a friend.

Can you perform well when you are in a high-pressure scenario?

There are going to be high-pressure scenarios in every work environment. Clearly, this task is going to be more important for a position like an ambulance driver rather than someone who might take down appointments at a spa. However, in even the most relaxing and casual jobs, you will still need to know how to handle a situation if things don't go completely as you expected.

Answer: I think I do well most of the time in these kinds of situations. Even when everything seems to be going wrong, I know how to take a step back and really find the right solution rather than letting myself become flustered. I have experience in helping calm people down and explaining the situation too so that others can feel the same way.

Is punctuality important to you?

Punctuality is going to be a hugely important aspect to look at for potential hiring managers. When someone needs you at a certain time, then they are clearly going to expect you to adhere to the time agreed upon. When you can't be punctual, it might indicate that you can't be reliable in other ways as well. You don't want to put yourself in a position where people won't depend on you, especially your employer. Being punctual means that you are more than just someone that shows up on time, you follow through with your word.

Answer: I believe punctuality is very important. There are times that some accidents might happen, which is why I ensure to try and always give myself more time than I need. You never really know what could happen. Being on time is also important because I know I get frustrated when I'm waiting for someone who is late, so I ensure that I don't do that to other people.

What are your biggest talents?

This is a question to see what skills you might possess outside of the workplace. Your answer will give insight into the kinds of things that are important to you, and what other talents you might bring that the person conducting the interview wasn't even looking for in the first place. It can add a little booster to your abilities, and you are showing that you are dedicated and valuable in ways not just related to your specific position.

Answer: I actually have the ability to draw rather well and come up with funny or quick catchphrases. I have an attention to detail, so even though it wasn't in the job description, I could help with social media management and create interesting content to help draw people in.

Who is your role model? Who is your biggest hero?

Your role model will reveal a lot about you. If you pick someone who is close to you, it shows you value the people closest to you on a different level. If you pick someone that is successful, it shows that you have high goals in life. Pick honestly and choose someone you legitimately look up to. Pick a general hero and try to stay away from a political figure or a religious figure.

Answer: While they might be a great role model in your eyes, it might be controversial for the person conducting the interview. Though it is discriminatory to not hire someone based on their religious or political views, it would be hard to prove that they did this since they didn't directly ask you the question. Keep it general and pick someone with strong values and respectable qualities. Describe them by their achievements and positive qualities that you think would be important to the specific job that you are applying for.

What is something that scares you?

This is a good question because it lets the person doing the interview know what about you might frighten you more than anything else. While you might not want them to know your weaknesses, remember that being afraid doesn't mean that you are weak. It's a good way to let them know that you do have things that you might be afraid of, but that you have healthily realized these fears. It will also be a way to share with them ways that you might be wanting to overcome your fears so that nothing holds you back.

Answer: I would have to say my biggest fear is probably not progressing further. I don't want to wake up one day later in life and be regretful that I wasn't doing as much as possible to give me the best life that I deserve. While it is not always easy to continue to move forward to strive for consistent grow all the time, I do still want to emphasize that I always do the most I can to keep getting closer and closer to my overall goals.

Who Inspires You?

To get to know a candidate, an interviewer may ask, who inspires you? This is a great question, because it reveals much about your character and values.

We all admire certain people. If a candidate says they admire someone because of their power or status, that can be a turn-off for an employer. On the other hand, if a candidate can respond with an answer that features someone with the same values as the interviewer's organization, it can demonstrate an outstanding fit for the candidate and the job.

Answer: I've always admired my mother. She was a nurse, and she was incredibly compassionate. She had a sense of pride because she was able to ease people's suffering.

Avoid talking about a celebrity or political figure because they can be polarizing, and if they don't share the values of the company, your example may alienate the interviewer.

Personal examples are typically best because the interviewer will have no preconceived notions about the person. You can focus on the attributes that most closely align with the organization's culture and values. If you've researched the organization, you should be able to connect your answer with those attributes.

Why Should I Hire You?

Give a clear example that shows why you're a better fit for the specific role than other people who are applying.

Answer: I understand that you're looking for someone who will research the marketplace and study consumers to identify business opportunities. I've demonstrated those skills when I was an Insights Analyst at Highbrow Salons. We were losing share because consumers were choosing smaller, niche salons. I researched the issue and identified a segmentation strategy that led to a new marketing approach. I then designed and executed the research plan that identified our new marketing message and social media strategy. That led to the company's first year of sales growth in over five years, and they've grown every year since they implemented the new campaign.

If you hire me, I'll bring that passion for growing a business and my skills for researching the marketplace to your team.

Why Did You Leave Your Last Job?

Employers might be curious about your reason for leaving jobs. They want to hire someone who will be around for a while, so be prepared to answer why you left each job that you've had.

Typically, we have a number of reasons for leaving a job, so focus on the reason that demonstrates that you'll be a better fit for your new job than you were for one of the jobs you left.

Good reasons for leaving jobs include wanting more responsibility, shifting your career direction to focus on something you have passion for, or moving to a new city for family reasons. These answers indicate that you have ambition, passion, or family ties to the location where you're job hunting.

Bad reasons include not liking the people you worked with, being bored with your job, or leaving because you just felt like making a change. With these answers, employers might see you as someone who is difficult to work with, easily dissatisfied, or cursed with a short attention span.

Answer: I have had three different jobs since graduating from high school. When I was getting my associates degree, I worked part-time as a personal care assistant for an elderly woman. I enjoyed that job, but it was not possible for it to become a full-time job when I graduated, so I left for a full-time position.

My next job was as an orderly at a hospital. I loved working with the patients and medical staff, but I wanted more responsibility, so I accepted a job as a medical assistant.

After working at that job for two years, my husband got transferred here to Cleveland. Therefore, I'm looking for medical assistant jobs here. I really love working as a medical assistant, and I'm excited to find a place in the area where I can make a contribution to the organization.

What sorts of books do you read?

The interviewer is trying to assess what interests you in books, are you a learner and do you read or not. This question can get very important if the job requires you to learn, do research or educate. If you do not read anything, you can come up with a nice answer of what takes up your time instead.

Answer: I love reading and my choice varies from fiction to scientific research books. The last book I read was X by ABC and I admire the writer for all the hard work that he has put in to his research.

Tell me your personal life.

Talking about your personal life seems a very easy task, because you are experiencing your life every single day and describing your life can hardly get wrong. However, to avoid raising red flags, your answers need to be prepared as well.

Answer: When answering this question, many people just use one sentence describing what they do. In fact, you have to dress up your saying, based on the Scenario-Attack-Outcome approach. Although responding by a sentence answers the question, responding by a story can better sell yourself to the interviewer. For example, you are volunteering in your son's school, where you organized the teacher appreciation week and all the teachers were happy with your preparations. You love campout during long weekends; you led a camping activity where you assigned family members with various duties for setting up a tent and barbecuing a lunch. You are a tennis lover, and publish a series of online videos teaching people how to play tennis. Your painting skills are excellent, and won a competition.

When you describe the personal life based on storytelling, your characteristics (e.g., leadership, detailed, etc.) show off as well. In some cases, the interviewer also infers your way of releasing high pressure from heavy workload. The characteristics are what the interviewer looks for.

Are you a big-picture person or a detail-oriented person?

A good answer has two aspects. First, every job has its orientation, so you need to know which style the job prefers. For instance, financial professionals, scientists, engineers, physicians, assistants, and researchers are better to be detailed. In general, the jobs involving quantitative or technologies are detail-oriented. In contrast, big-picture jobs require strategic and creative thinking; examples include upper management teams, consultants, entrepreneurs, writers, musicians, and counselors.

Second, the answer better covers both styles, with an emphasis on the job's need. For example, you may say I am a big-picture/detail-oriented person most of time, but also can grasp the details/goals when necessary. Basically, it is hard for the interviewer to know how you encompass both styles in the work. Giving a Scenario-Attack-Outcome story is highly recommended. For instance, a choir conductor is a big-picture job, but the conductor also needs a detailed plan to lead the singers to practice a song.

If you can restart your career, what would you do differently?

Answer: When your work history shows an obvious issue (e.g., being laid off, a short working period for a job), it is a time to address the situation. You can briefly describe the scenario, but the **lessons** you learned are more important. Your answer should further focus on describing the lessons. In principle, if you are unable to hide the bad history, your answer is to turn any issues into motivation that drives you to become a better employee in the future.

If your career has no problem at all, your answer should express your satisfaction about whatever you have done. You are pleased with the direction you have taken. There is nothing to regret. You would redo everything identically.

What would your ultimate dream job be?

Your dream job might be to lay on the beach and have people pay you to do nothing all day but eat delicious snacks. You can say this if you want, but they will really be wanting to know what type of personality you have. Be truthful and apply it to the job while also refrain from obviously schmoozing them.

Answer: My dream position would be one where I can have creative freedom while also having a team around me that can help support me with my accountability deadlines, or someone that offers creative perspectives when I'm stuck. I would want a changing environment where I could grow, but one that is also reliable that I know I will have around because job security is important to me.

How do you motivate yourself when you feel like you don't want to do anything?

Motivation is a key factor in many positions. The person conducting the interview will simply want to know how you are able to motivate yourself even when you feel like you want to do nothing at all.

Answer: Motivation is best when it comes from within myself. I'll usually try to reward myself. Maybe if I get a project done early then I'll go out for lunch rather than eating what I already packed. If I can't find that motivation within myself, then I like talking to friends and family who encourage me to keep going, or I might listen to some of my favorite songs or read cheesy quotes that help to inspire me!

If you could change one thing about your appearance, what would it be? If you could change something about your personality, what would it be?

This is a tricky question that might throw you off, but it's also a fun one that gives the person conducting the interview an idea of how you think. What is it that you think is the most important thing to change about your physical appearance? What about your personality? It's going to be important that you are self-aware and understanding of what issues you might need to improve on. You also don't want to be too harsh on yourself.

Answer: If I could change one thing about my appearance, I would probably want to whiten my teeth! I think a bright smile is important for spreading positivity and showing that I'm friendly. For my personality, I would also want to be less critical and nicer to myself so that I have more confidence.

Can you describe a time when you really learned your lesson, or had an enlightening moment that you still frequently apply to your current life?

The person conducting the interview is not going to expect that you are perfect. What they will be the most concerned about is that even if you do have a flaw, you know exactly what you need to do to fix it. They want to know that whatever issues you might have, you have the ability to recognize what needs to be learned from the situation and that you had learned the lesson. Life is not about regretting your mistakes; it's about learning from them.

Answer: There was one time when I found myself very stressed out from work on Friday to the point that I couldn't enjoy my weekend because I had so much to do on Monday. I had a fun trip planned that was completely ruined by my anxiety over work on Monday. I learned that it was most important for me to get my work done on time so that I could enjoy my time off work more.

Can you describe yourself in three words or less?

This is a common question that will likely be asked frequently, but it's also a hard one that you might struggle to come up with answers to! Don't overthink it. Think about keywords that might have been in the job description, which can help you better determine what they might be looking for. Include a professional trait, a real authentic trait, and one that is related to your personality – who you really are deep down. Rather than give you an exact answer, here are some keywords that you likely have, but will also help to make you sound great:

- Reliable

- Trustworthy

- Funny

- Logical

- Positive

- Practical

If you had to pick a career completely unrelated to this field, what would it be?

This is a fun question that many employers will want to hear from you. If you weren't doing what you are doing, what would you be doing in a nutshell? If you are working a retail job to help you get through college while you are studying to become a nurse, then you would probably tell them that you want to be a nurse since that's your eventual goal. However, take this opportunity to be creative if you want and share what you would consider completely unrelated to anything that you are a part of.

Answer: Being a financial advisor is what I want to do now, but I always had dreams of being a veterinarian. I would have considered this field, but blood and surgery makes me queasy so I don't think I would have lasted long! I still love animals, but I understand now that my true talents lie within this field.

Do you enjoy morning or night better?

This is good to know specifically to the job that you are interviewing for, but it also reveals a little bit about who you are. If you are a morning person but interviewing for the night shift, of course, cater your answer, but also reveal a little bit more about why you might be a morning or a night person.

Answer: I would have to say that I'm more of a night person. While I love mornings, I also get excited to experience new things on a night out like restaurants and bars. I definitely have an easier time staying up late than waking up early in the morning.

What kinds of jokes do you find to be the funniest?

Sense of humor is essential for many positions. While you might not necessarily be applying for a position that requires your comedic skills, it's still nice to have someone with a good sense of humor working in the office. If you have a funny joke that you like to share, now is the time to do that, as long as it's appropriate, of course. Give them a little insight into what your sense of humor is like and what they could expect from you if hired.

Answer: I would describe my sense of humor as being pretty diverse. I laugh easily and love watching funny videos or looking at pictures. I'm more of someone who laughs easily at myself rather than get easily offended, though I might not always be the one to be making most of the jokes. I love sharing funny ideas and it's always fun to get to know what someone else thinks is funny as well.

What is a skill that someone you know has, that you wish that you had yourself? What do you envy about those that you admire?

This question will be to showcase what you might be able to see in the people around you, and the type of things that you value the most. It will give your potential employer an idea of the things that you will want to improve on, and also give them a sense of the kind of things that you pay attention to. Be honest with this, but not superficial. Don't state that you like someone else's hair, their body, or their style. Instead, discuss how they might have a crafty eye, a good sense of what's popular, or heightened confidence that you admire.

Answer: I have a friend that I know who is seemingly fearless. He can walk into any room at any time and make friends with the grumpiest and meanest looking person. I envy his confidence at times and wish that I had that trait. He's definitely helped me to come out of my shell, and though I might never be as confident, I still do my best to keep up with his charisma.

If you woke up tomorrow a completely different person, what three things would you miss the most about your life?

This is a question that will help to determine what it is that you like about your life the most. The interview process can teach you to be rather critical, so this is a good reminder to talk about the things that you really enjoy including in your daily life.

Answer: If I woke up tomorrow a completely different person, the first thing I would miss would be all the loved ones that I have in my life. After that, I would miss the experiences that I had gone through. I would worry that I'd be a different person had I not gone through what I did. Finally, the third thing that I would miss would probably be all the stuff that I had been collecting over the years!

What is your philosophy towards work?

Answer: Tell the interviewer, what kind of a worker are you (your positive qualities as a worker), the reason why you work, the passion you have toward the position or the company you are applying, etc. for example: I will work hard for my professional development as well as the development of the company.

To work hard, to share and learn knowledge for and from the co-workers, to work sincerely and honestly, to apply what I have learnt for the benefit of many people, etc.

What do you usually do in your leisure time?

Tell them about your hobbies. Make it clear that your hobbies will not distract your concentration from your job, but will give valuable contribution to your job.

Answer: I love playing tennis because it maintains my physical being as well as decreases my stress, so that I can return to my professional routine with new energy.

What have you done to improve your capacities, knowledge, or yourself?

Answer: Give examples including trainings, seminars, conferences, workshops, peer learning, supervisor-subordinate learning, self-learning, etc.

CHAPTER 2: SKILLS AND COMPETENCES QUESTIONS

What did you do in your last job and how was your experience?

An easy question. Explain briefly your job responsibilities and experience should be put in a friendly tone. Negative sentences can damage your impression.

Answer: As a XYZ, my key responsibilities were xxxx. My experience as a XYZ in ABC Company was really good. I found the management and my colleagues very helpful and friendly. That is the environment they keep. Overall it was a great experience working with such a nice and knowledgeable staff.

Describe one incidence when you made a suggestion and it failed

The best way is to answer with some project where your time assessment was not correct. This answer is harmless as you could narrate any incidence where you assessed wrongly but then you learnt from it.

Answer: I once made a project schedule, which was pretty tough but I thought I could make it in time. Some unprecedented problem arrived and it changed the entire schedule. I took responsibility for the failure and promised to myself that I would not schedule things this way again.

What's your management style?

An answer to this question consists of two parts: **philosophy** and **examples**. Good management style includes dynamic, flexible, open-minded, and encouraging. In other words, you do not always stick to a same way to handle your team; your management style should be able to implement different strategies dependent on contexts; you can accept different opinions from your team; you can motivate or encourage your team to work for you; you treat yourself as a teacher when leading your team.

Answer: Giving examples based on the Scenario-Attack-Outcome approach is important in your answer. If you used to be a manager, telling a good story should be easy. If you never played a managerial role in past jobs, you can use examples in your extracurricular or volunteering activities. Alternatively, although you never served as a manager, your experiences in leading a project can be included in your answer. Regardless, any example showing that you exerted your leadership in a project is a good story.

Can you remember a time in the past where you came up with a new idea or unexpected solution to a group issue?

Your interviewer will likely enjoy throwing a lot of curveball questions like this one at you. They want to see if you can handle responding quickly and professionally in a way that allows you to showcase a legitimate experience you had in your past jobs.

Answer: At my last job, we struggled to get a lot of foot traffic into the store, and not many people drove by the corner bakery I was employed. I noticed that the Laundromat next-door was frequently busy, and every so often, we would get people coming in while they did their laundry. My manager struggled to find marketing ways to bring people in, but I suggested that we offered a 10% discount to anyone that came in from the Laundromat. He was skeptical at first, but after trying it out for a week, business rapidly increased. People who wouldn't have come in otherwise ended up becoming returning customers.

What qualities do you admire in those who held previous leadership positions that you have worked with? Can you describe a boss that you looked up to?

Interviewers will ask you this because they want to know what you might see in others that are good qualities to have in your working life. They want to figure out if you notice these kinds of things and gauge if you can pick up on the good qualities of others and use them yourself. Think back to someone you liked, even if it was a teacher, and determine what it was about them that made them a good leader. This specific response will end up being one that gives them insight as to what qualities you believe a manager should hold.

Answer: I had a manager at one of my jobs who was always bringing us things she baked, sending us happy birthday texts, and making sure that we had enough days off a month to really get some time to relax. I admired here because she went above and beyond to make sure that she appreciated us not just as workers, but as people too. It helped me and my coworkers feel more valued, and for that, we took great pride in the work that we did.

Can you describe a time when you made a genuine mistake, and what did you do to fix this?

Everyone makes mistakes, and it would be silly to pretend as though every candidate is free of these mistakes during any interview. The person asking the questions will likely choose this one because they want to know if you are able to recognize your mistakes. Not only that, but they want to know that you know how to fix these issues when they are presented to you.

Answer: When I was 18, I failed a few classes, changed my major twice, and dropped out of school for a year. It was a total mistake, or so I thought at the time. I fell behind my other classmates and felt like a loser. However, this time off ended up giving me the clarity to figure out exactly what I wanted to do, and I took a long enough break that when I went back, I felt comfortable with the subjects I chose, making it easier to maintain good grades. What I thought was a mistake turned into the realization that I needed to discover more about myself and my future.

Can you adjust quickly to a rapidly changing environment? Would you be able to change your plans if something unexpected happened?

There may be a time when your employer has to send you to a different location, or perhaps they need you to work in a different department, depending on your skills and the versatility of management. It is up to you, then, to make sure that you know how to adapt should a situation like this occur. Be honest with them and let them know if you are going to be able to quickly adapt to situations like this if that's what you have to do later on.

Answer: I have no problem trying new things. I appreciate having a set schedule so that I know what needs to be done, but when things change, it can just make work feel more exciting, making going to work more enjoyable. I'm not concerned about my abilities to adapt should there be a situation when I need to quickly adjust to change.

What strong organizational skills do you have?

Being organized is incredibly important. They can simply ask, do you have this skill, or this skill, or this skill, and so on, but instead, they are leaving this question for you to fill in the blanks. Rather than blatantly stating that you are detail oriented, punctual, and so on, put an emphasis on sharing your actual steps to become organized so that they can have a better sense of whether or not you are really someone with a great set of organization skills.

Answer: I think organization is incredibly important in order to avoid any issues that might arise during any given project. To get organized, I first make a list of all the tasks that I need to do. From there, I will prioritize them by importance and separate them by how much time they will take and look at ways that I might be able to complete two tasks simultaneously. From there, I do my best to adhere to timelines, always giving myself a little extra time to account for any incidents that might occur!

What drew you into this particular field of work in the first place?

Sometimes we interview for jobs that align with our ultimate dream positions. Other times, these jobs are nothing more than a placeholder to help pay the bills while we really work on what our dreams are. Regardless, you will likely be asked a question about your interest in the field in general, not just your interest in the position. Be honest! There is always a reason. Even if you want to be a lawyer but applied at a dog hotel, you would have still had a passion for dogs that helped you to choose that over something else.

Answer: I chose this field because it interests me. I'm passionate about learning more, and I also feel as though it can help me grow. I also have experience in this position, so I feel as though it is easier for me to fit in with a company like this.

How Soon Could You Make an Impact?

An interviewer might ask this question to see if you're prepared to hit the ground running. They may need immediate results, and they want you to tell them that you're prepared to deliver.

Answer: I plan to have an impact immediately. Since I've been an event planner in this area for seven years, I know the local venues and agencies well. I took the liberty of preparing a 30-60-90 Day Plan to show you how I might approach the role if you hire me.

Describe circumstances where you had to work under pressure and deal with deadlines.

Answer: This should be an easy one for everyone, but do not take it for granted. Consider your best, most recent story that the interviewer is most likely to relate to. If this is the essence of your daily activities, mention that fact and discuss the various deadlines and pressures you need to deal with on a regular and daily basis. This is as true, if not even more so, for those returning to the workplace. With many projects to deal with and soft lines of responsibility, the pressure may be greater and the deadlines sometimes ignored until a crisis develops.

If you cannot think of such a situation either at work or in your personal life, seek assistance from a relative, friend, or colleague. The experiences are there; it just takes sensitivity to identify them.

How do you rate your expertise?

Answering this question typically relies on a **numeric rating**. You need to begin with your defined score range; e.g., 1 is the worst, and 100 is the best, followed by assigning a score based on your personal viewpoint.

Answer: When the position you are applying is a manager of a professional team (e.g., a manager of scientists, a manager of programmers, a manager of accountants, etc.), answer strategy is a bit tricky. Since your role consists of management and professional knowledge, you may choose to give two scores, one on each aspect. In this scenario, the score on your professional knowledge should be very high; otherwise, you are not able to lead the team. As for the management score, you should rate at least above average.

What is a challenging decision in a work environment that you have had to make?

The person conducting the interview is going to want to know if you are good with ultimatums, dilemmas, and debates. Do you have what it takes to know whether or not what you are choosing to do is right? Are you sure of yourself and confident once you have made a final decision? This is what you might answer this question with:

Answer: One time at work, I had to decide between two girls that had requested the same day off. Someone had to work, but both needed time off, so I was faced with the dilemma of deciding who to grant the vacation request to. Both were great girls, and they had high levels of performance. Ultimately, I decided to look at the past records of who might have asked for time off more. One girl had never requested a leave in the two years that she was there, whereas the other girl requested a weekend off at least once a month. I ended up scheduling the girl who requested for more time off regularly but she worked half of her shift, so she still got off early to enjoy the time off.

What is something that you used to struggle with, but since have grown from?

Not everyone is perfect all the time, and it's unrealistic to expect that this could be the case. Your employers are only going to know who you are from the time that you start working with them. They want insight into your background, so they'll be asking questions like these to try and get a sneak peek at who you used to be before stumbling into this position. This is something that you might respond with:

Answer: I used to have trouble speaking my mind. I was passive because I wanted to keep the peace. I've since learned that not only does it make me feel better to express myself and share the truth, but it helps to improve communication with me and other people and gives us the chance to find a better solution than if I had just left the decision up to them.

Why is it important to achieve more and go beyond just the minimum requirements?

We should always be doing more than just the bare minimum. When we only do what we have to, then that sets the standard for our work. Come up with your own unique answer for this question, but this is also something that you might consider saying if you were asked this:

Answer: When you choose to go above and beyond, then you are showing that you put effort into your work. You show pride and integrity, and that you have great reliability and are trustworthy. I also find this is beneficial because if there ever is a moment where I don't perform my best, then I can at least show from my work history that I am usually efficient and that this was just a one-time situation where I was a little off in my performance.

What has been your greatest achievement in life? What about in your career?

This question is usually asked because they want to know what your biggest accomplishment is. Think about what has been the single most important time in your life or something that you are proud of to share with others. They want to see your passion as you talk and find out how you might have been able to improve your   own   life. Make sure that when you share this you give a personal or a career related answer, depending on how they might end up asking.

Answer: My greatest achievement was certainly getting my Master's degree. Before I even applied to graduate school, I was nervous. I thought I wouldn't be able to do well because I had a bad semester as an undergrad. I let this become my source of motivation and graduated at the top of my class! Whenever I doubt myself I don't use my degree as a reminder, but instead, my dedication that was required for all the hours of studying and homework to remind me of all the things that I'm capable of.

What are your career goals?

You could come up with short term and long term goals whatever you choose if not asked specifically. Your goals should involve achieving the company's vision and help it grow. But an entry level person saying that he aims to becoming the company's CEO would sound too much. Be reasonable and even if you aim big, your timing matters a lot.

Answer: I want to excel in my field and then move within the company to learn about other departments and fields. Once I become a master in all, I would want to pursue my career in management as leadership comes natural to me.

Who was your worst supervisor?

Do not say anything bad about any ex employer/ boss/ colleague. This just goes on to damage your image and your chances of nailing this job. You could come up with other ways of describing your tough supervisors by saying words like challenging, perfectionist etc.

Answer: I will not say I had any bad supervisors, but yes I have had a few challenging ones. Meeting up to their demands had always been really tough but when I look back at things now, I realize that the tough time they gave me actually taught me how to manage stress and produce results. So I would say my experience with them was that of learning and grooming.

Do you prefer working in a team or alone?

A good answer is to say you are comfortable with both styles. However, this answer is a minimum, and it should be followed by expressing your preference. Note that the preference is not based on your personal desire, but based on what the job needs.

In spite that you are a highly independent person, you need to lean towards being collaborative when the job (e.g., project manager, human resource specialist, flight attendant, etc.) requires more team work. Furthermore, working in a team requires your **flexibility**, since team members have different characteristics.

Answer: When the job (e.g., accountant, attorney, programmer, etc.) requires you to work alone most of time, your answer should demonstrate your independent thinking capability. Moreover, your answer also expresses that you are a **detailed** person able to identify and fix errors. On the other hand, your answer should mention that you also enjoy the benefits of working with other members, because you like to learn other people's ideas or hear their feedback.

Another trick is to acquire more information from the interviewer. For example, after you answer I'm comfortable with both styles, you may further ask About how much time do you think will be spent doing work independently vs. collaboratively? Or, Does the company encourage one style over the other one? Based on the interviewer's response, you can follow his logic to square up your answer.

What will be the ideal job for you?

You should not be specific while answering this question. Make a general statement like the one given below to be suitable to almost all kinds of jobs.

Answer: My ideal job would be one which allows me utilize my professional and personal skills in the best possible way. I am happy with a job that offers growth and provides me room to make positive contributions.

Show me how you are good at handling multitasking

The interviewer is perhaps trying to assess if you can handle the load of work by multitasking. How will you handle several urgent tasks at a time? Do not give the impression that you multitask all the time since it breaks your total attention towards a single piece of work. This can also affect your quality of work.

Answer: I can multitask if the need arises. If there are a few urgent things coming up demanding my attention at once then I stretch myself to manage them within the allowed time constraints.

How did you choose this line of profession?

Your answer should make sense. You chose a particular line because you wanted to grow professionally in that fashion. For example, studying Mechanical Engineering because you wanted to build and design engines etc.

Answer: I chose Software engineering because I was interested in the automation of things.

What is your role in a team? What role would you play if you were in a leadership position?

We already talked about what your leadership or follower status, but it's also crucial that you remember where you might fit in the team overall. Would you be the listener? The judge? The mediator? The organizer? Think of all the roles that there could possibly be within any given team and determine where you might feel the most comfortable.

Answer: I believe that I would be somewhat of a mediator. I have a good sense of knowing what is right and what is wrong, and I often look for ways that more than one person can get their needs met at a time. When we focus on the group as a whole, we can discover the best solutions possible meaning that everyone will thrive. It's easy for me to play the role of the devil's advocate and I don't mind helping resolve issues between two people.

Tell us about your achievements.

Answer: It could be your academic achievements or non-academic achievements (sports, arts, music, etc.). If you do not have any, you can mention simple things that were big contributions to your life. For example: When you defeated your fear and did your best to achieve your goals. Or, when you failed but then did not give up and gave your biggest efforts until you succeed.

In your opinion what is the most challenging aspect of the last role that you have played?

This is another one of the team playing assessment questions. You should be prepared for questions about your past history like this. Do mention teamwork at least once in your answer. Try remembering a situation, which got resolved and highlight the role you played while working as a team.

Answer: The most challenging aspect of my last job was to manage and motivate my staff so that their focus remained undeterred.

How do you normally interact with coworkers?

Some environments will be completely isolated, and you won't have to talk to a soul. Others will require complete collaboration. This is a good question to help the person asking to know whether or not you will be able to work well with the rest of the team. Be honest, if you have friends from previous positions, that's great! If you struggled to mingle, share why.

Answer: I can be shy at first, sometimes afraid to let others get to know me, but once I've found my footing and become comfortable, it's easy for me to open up and make friends. Getting along with others is important to me so that I can enjoy my work that much more, and it makes the job a lot more fun as well.

Are you a good team player?

Nobody would want to hire you otherwise. The interviewer actually wants to assess your interpersonal skills. Narrating an incident where you came to a compromise with a colleague who was creating conflict within a team would be perfect.

Answer: I remember when we were being trained for our first market experience one of my team mates was consistently asking questions that made no sense. He was not only wasting time but was also frustrating the other team members who were eagerly trying to concentrate on the training. I asked the trainers to conduct some team building games and after some time I found that the troublesome colleague of mine was actually helping out others! My trick had worked and his mind was taken off from asking nonsensical questions.

Walk Me through Your Resume

Walk me through your resume is almost identical to Tell me about yourself. You can use the P-E-N framework for both questions.

Answer: For this question, I like to see candidates summarize each section of their resume by providing highlights from the Education and Experience sections. Typically, it's best to provide a chronological summary of your most relevant experiences.

Avoid the temptation to read your resume. The interviewer doesn't want you to recite things that they can read themselves. They want you to tell them the highlights in your own words.

What development tools are you familiar with?

Your answer should be relevant to your line of interest. You should have experience of using the latest and the most frequent/ commonly used tools. However never bluff and say you know what you actually don't. But prepare yourself before coming so that even if you have not used some latest tool, you have an idea of its working and functionality.

Answer: I am currently using xxxx. I also have hands on experience of using xxxx.

Tell me something about your best project.

This question is very easy and straightforward. Your best project should be something in which you did an extra ordinary thing. Your contribution should have made the best contribution in the project. You could share a project that gave excellent results, made the management happy or made you proud that you put in the extra bit.

Answer: I remember that just two days prior to our company's annual day, one of our major products failed in the final testing. It could have been a great disaster as it was already being commercialized in the market and was to be launched at the annual function. I collaborated with a few teams and we decided that a few of us from each team would stay at office until the product gets the clearance. It was the evening of the launch day when the product passed its final testing and we all took a breath of relief. The management applauded us for the extra effort and compensated with a bonus for each team.

What measures do you take to control quality?

This question could be answered as following for the job of Quality Controller/ Quality Assurance/ Analyst etc. The answer could also be used in some other technical fields where international quality standards are kept in focus.

Answer: I will follow company's policy and procedures to make sure my work falls in line with them. I will also assess my work against the current practices for quality control to deliver a high quality end product.

Explain what you did in your last job. What were your major job responsibilities?

The interviewer is now interested in your technical/ work relevant skills. Your past experience should support the future role that you are trying to pursue. Like if you supervised a team, you could apply for a managerial post as you have experience of team leading.

Answer: I have worked for the past three years in Warid Telecom as an MNP Supervisor. My major job responsibilities were xxxx.

Have you ever faced a team conflict? What role did you play?

The key to resolving conflict in a team is to finding common grounds and then agreeing on it. If you say you never had a conflict, then you appear as a person who cannot voice his opinion. Try to narrate an incidence where you had an opinion, which was conflicting with the opinions of a few other team members. You should try remembering a situation and not try and fabricate one.

Answer: When you are working in a team, conflict is unavoidable. I remember this one time when our boss asked us to come up with an idea of how to xxxx. All of us had different opinions but then we narrowed down to two. We could not agree on which one idea to put forward.

If you faced a problem with a colleague, how would you deal with it?

This is another one of the team player skills assessment questions. Be truthful and positive. Having trouble with a colleague does not mean that you have to bad mouth anyone. If you are working in a team, conflict will surely arise. Difference of opinion is one reasonable way of answering this question.

Answer: In my current job, there is one person in my team who always has a different opinion on things than mine. We almost always have a different approach; he puts more focus on the bigger picture whilst I try to put in some practicality. When we try to come on common grounds, we always have the best solution to problems. Even though we are not friends but we get along great as a team.

Can you tell me about a time where you went above and beyond and did even more than what you were expected to do?

This is a hard question because it will put you on the spot. Employers still want to see if you can come up with information like this quickly and without another prompt. Though challenging, you will still want to have a specific example so that they can truly see the nature of your character. You will want to pull preferably from a time period when you were working somewhere else. Don't lie and make yourself sound extra good – they will be able to tell. Be honest and speak from experience because it will be easier to remember this event when it comes time to talk about it then. Describe not just how you were able to go beyond what you were asked to do, but how you also managed to help the business out in some way as well. This would be a good answer, but remember to keep it specific to the scenario and not to base it verbatim of ours:

Answer: There was a time when I used to work at the ice cream store in my hometown. At night, it would be our duty to clean the place up and then clock out. The morning staff would be responsible for setting up for the next day. One night we were rather slow, so I decided to do all of the morning prep. The next day, the workers came in and didn't have to do much at all, making their morning start off easier. On top of that, they were able to open early and let some people in the store who had already been waiting.

How would your last boss, manager, or supervisor describe you as an employee?

This is another great question that they will likely ask you in some form or other. They want to know not just what you are like as an employee, but as someone who takes orders from the higher-ups. Were you feared by them? Did they have trouble telling you things? Were they your best friend? This previous relationship with the higher-ups will be important in helping them see what benefits you might bring to the position as an employee.

Answer: I would say that I had a pretty good relationship with my last supervisor. We had open communication and instead of her always telling me what to do, we worked together to delegate tasks that I was better at to me and delegate tasks that she was better at to her, always checking in with each other to make sure both of our needs were being met.

Can you describe to me a time in the past at a different position in which you were faced with a very challenging scenario, and what you did in the moment to resolve the issue?

This is a good question where your answer will show that you are recognizing what you might have struggled with in the past, and how you handle pressure when you are faced with an obstacle.

Remember to stay honest, and don't feel the need to go into every last agonizing detail about this.

Answer: There was a time when I worked retail at a small gift shop. I noticed that a woman was stuffing some smaller jewelry pieces into her purse. She was standing right by the door, so I feared that she was going to make a run for it. I asked her if she needed any help and showed her some merchandise at the back of the store to buy me time while I talked to the owner. She was about to leave when I asked her if she was going to pay for the items in her purse. After retrieving the items, the owner and I decided to let her go since it was less than $30 worth of merchandise, but we made sure she wasn't allowed back in. I panicked at first and wanted to stop her immediately, but that could have turned into a messy situation, so I tried to remain as calm as possible and work with my supervisor to find the right solution.

What is something that you saw a different employee do that you wouldn't do yourself? Can you describe a time when a coworker did something they shouldn't do? How did you handle this?

This question might be phrased in a few different ways, but it's an important one that will give them insight into what you believe a good employee should be like. There are a ton of employees who do the wrong thing, so when you can show that you recognize the difference between right and wrong, it makes you all the more trustworthy. Don't shame anyone, don't use names, and make sure that you aren't being rude. Simply state what they did wrong, why it was wrong, and how you would have corrected the situation.

Answer: There was a time in my last job when my coworker would always leave her leftover tasks for the person that came into the next shift. Even though she worked a slower shift, there would still be leftover tasks that she didn't bother to complete. Initially, I confronted her about it. I made sure all my tasks were done and left a note asking to help out during the slow shifts since ours were busier at night. She ended up ignoring this, so I had a discussion with my boss, and we came up with the perfect task list that fairly delegated the right amount of duties.

How did you take leave today from your current job?

You could be honest about it if you actually told your current employer about the interview. But just don't say that you told them you were sick or something like that.

Answer: I took an unpaid off today as taking leaves otherwise consumes more time.

What was your worst experience in the previous job?

Your worst experience should never relate to even a minor requirement in the job you are applying for. Sometimes you cannot judge that so be careful while answering. Your answer should be as harmless as could be. You could say there was not much opportunity for growth, your skills were not being properly used or you wanted to look for newer challenges as the job was not testing your talent.

Answer: My experience at my previous position was great. My colleagues and supervisors were all very supportive and friendly. I really enjoyed my time there. The only problem was that I did not find the job challenging enough. I felt my skills were not being used properly and so I am looking for newer more challenging opportunities.

What expectations do you have from supervisors?

You could put forward your preferences and it is best if you answer according to the

Company's current working practice. If the company supports the idea of a one to one connection between the supervisor and the subordinate, then the following answer would be great.

Answer: I prefer working in a friendly environment where juniors can interact freely with their supervisors.

What will your ex employers say about you?

You could bring up your best personal and professional traits by mentioning that others will remember you by them. Again it is preferable if your answer include something that will help you perform your current job role.

Answer: They will definitely remember me as hard working, devoted, friendly and honest.

Why did you opt for studying in XYZ University?

There is nothing much technical to this question. You can hardly be wrong in answering this one. The key is: just be prepared to answer. You should know the pluses of your university and why you preferred it over others. If your reason is a lame one like my friends applied and so did I then do not answer that. Your answer should limelight the good points of your university.

Answer: XYZ is considered among the top engineering universities of the country. In certain areas it is considered the best in Asia. Established in the 1850's, this university is producing the most intelligent and brilliant engineers than any other engineering university. It is the dream of every aspiring engineer to be studied from this university.

How were you as a student?

Answer this honestly and if you were not a bright student, then very tactfully. The employer could check you out, and any big words can get you in trouble. Tell about the best subjects where you scored, earned an award or your teacher appreciated you etc.

Answer: I was a real hardworking student. I was excellent in xxxx and xxxx. My teachers many a times during viva would say that I was very intelligent. I wanted to excel in all subjects but xxxx came naturally to me. I was not the topper in my class but my teachers knew me because of the hard work and effort that I put in.

What will your teachers say about you?

You can put yourself in the right light by answering with your best traits. Try remembering how your teachers had praised you at any time.

Answer: My teachers would say that I was very attentive, had excellent participation in class, was friendly and had a good sense of humor.

What were your most favorite subjects?

Be honest and tell your favorite subjects. You need to be truthful about it since you could be questioned according to what you answer. It seems like an easy question but you could get trapped if you had little knowledge of the subject you say as your favorite.

Answer: My favorite subjects were xxxx and xxxx.

What was the best time of your educational time?

Nothing much technical about this question but preparing for this will help you answer it more confidently. Your best time could be any educational achievement, any activity or any help or assistance that you might have provided.

Answer: I got rolled in the University of XYZ to learn from the most knowledgeable professors of my time and the day I got my degree was certainly the most rewarding moment of my entire educational time.

What did you like about your most favorite teacher?

Try remembering your most favorite teacher; how he/ she taught and what you liked about him/ her the most.

Answer: Mr. XYZ was not only my most favorite teacher but the whole University loved him. He was always willing to help and was easily approachable. He actually wanted to transfer his knowledge to his students unlike other teachers who were just doing their jobs. He was a humble genius and the students had great respect for him. No doubt, the students showed extra ordinary results in his subjects.

Is your study relevant to what you want to be professionally?

Of course. It should be. If not directly then find relevance as to how it should help you in finding the right job for you. Your studies should help you polish your skills required for your future jobs.

Answer: I have done XYZ in xxxx, which is what is required for performing job as a xxxx. My academic tenure has helped me polish my skills so that I am able to work along with the best in my field.

Tell me about your extracurricular activities.

The interviewer may be trying to judge your social skills. Are you a team player or a loner? How confident are you?

Answer: I was president of a computer society of my University. We organized events and award ceremonies to encourage students to bring out their best. Apart from that I was also a part of tennis, cricket and swimming teams.

Do you want to study further?

It depends upon the job whether you want to study or not. If the job requires consistent learning, taking courses etc, then of course you want it. But if it requires you to gain experience and studying further would mean quitting this job then your answer should be a definite no.

Answer: Yes, I would definitely study further to contribute more for my organization with new

How do you make sure that you achieve your projected targets?

You could answer this question generally in the following manner. However, if your job role requires you to do a little more than that mentioned as following then make your answer more relevant.

Answer: First of all, I segregate the entire project and give a separate schedule for each segment. It becomes easy to manage and track time that way. Then keeping close follow-ups and proper feedbacks, I have always managed to achieve my projected targets.

How would you establish credibility in a team?

To establish credibility, you need to **produce outcomes** in your new job. Producing good outcomes relies on your understandings in the job tasks. Once you have a good understanding, an action plan should be carried out, e.g., which people you have to talk to, what actions you plan to take, what resources you hope to obtain, what skills you have to sharpen, what your clients care the most, etc.

Answer: Typically, the first 2–4 weeks are dedicated to knowing the company, culture, collaborative colleagues, external partners, and computer system. The following 2 months are spent in creating a detailed roadmap. Next, you will spend additional 2 months in executing the actions based on the roadmap, and hopefully some outcomes are generated. Then, the outcomes may prompt you to adjust your execution plan. Therefore, an execution plan covering 3–6 months is reasonable for answering this interview question.

Are you a risky person to have in our company?

Answer: This one mainly consists of what your previous jobs were, and why you left them. Tell them in a professional manner why, and you will show them why you left these other engagements. If it was because you were laid off, tell them that, but also talk about how your previous experiences will still great.

What's the ideal workplace for you?

Answer: This question is sure to see if you'll fit into the company. You can tell them honestly how you feel, and you can also compliment the work atmosphere of the job you're trying to get. This will definitely incite interest in the interviewer.

Tell me a successful project in your work.

Answer: Answering this question can take the strategy of answering the greatest achievement. Pick a past project that is most relevant to the job opportunity, and use the SAO approach to describe the task, the difficulties, and how you developed your solutions. Furthermore, don't forget to give the good results of the project. Since this project was successful, **the outcome is better described by a quantitative measure**; otherwise, you have to further explain why you think the project was successful or how the success was defined.

Tell me a failed project in your work. (What was your failure experience in the last job?)

Answer: People do not like failures or mistakes. However, people grow by making mistakes. When a toddler learns to walk, the kid must have fallen many times. A professor's manuscripts do not always get accepted every time he submits for review. The conversion rate of a sales pitch is never 100%. In fact, failures lay a foundation for future successes, so you should have learned some lessons from the failures. The lumps and bumps teach you what you should keep an eye on in order to avoid the same difficulties or mistakes. On a positive side, failures may become a helping force driving you towards success.

Describe your work style.

Answer: The style described in your answer should be a way to **streamline a work flow**. Typically, a style has two sides; for example, teamwork vs. independent; organized vs. disorganized; data driven vs. qualitative inference; creative vs. rule following; multi-tasking vs. solo-tasking; computer based vs. paper based; planning vs. execution; flexible working hours vs. regular 9am-5pm. Therefore, you need to understand the nature of the job opportunity, and choose a work style best fitting the job.

Some styles (e.g., well-organized) are good for all kinds of jobs. However, some styles are suitable for specific jobs only; e.g., engineers, accountants, and financial professionals are more data-driven. On the other hand, both collaboration and independence are required in most jobs, because people should be able to collaborate with other team members but independently complete some portions.

How was your working relationship with your previous boss?

The answer should show your **positive views** regarding your previous supervisor. Your answer should not contain a complaint. A stereotypic answer is: My previous boss was a great mentor, and I learned a lot from him. This answer shows you had a great relationship, and you are a good learner as well. Of course, you better use a Scenario-Attack-Outcome story to elaborate the relationship.

Answer: When you had a bad relationship with your past boss, you should avoid directly saying Our relationship was bad. A better way to answer is, for instance, our personalities were very different, so sometimes I had a hard time with him. However, working with him also transformed me to an adaptive person in my work style. Another example is: The supervisor and I had different training and experiences. His degree was in finance and mine was in marketing, so we frequently had different viewpoints. But eventually I could accept his opinions or he could agree my suggestions.

Did you have a bad experience in working with your supervisor?

Remember, you are in an interview, rather than chewing the fat! Your answer should never badmouth people. Even though you had a horrible experience, giving details of the experience in an interview will make you look ugly.

Answer: Ideally, your story starts with an introduction by saying Our personalities were very different, or preferably saying Our education backgrounds were different, so we sometimes looked at things from different perspectives. When you give such an introduction, the interviewer already has a sense: It is quite common in a workplace.

When you tell the main body of your story, don't give details of how you fought against your old boss. Your emphasis is directed to that the distinct opinions resulted from different trainings, educations or personalities.

How did you handle heavy workload?

Answer: You always have to prioritize critical tasks, negotiation with colleagues, or seek other people's help. In addition, don't forget to show your Scenario-Attack-Outcome stories which demonstrate your experiences in handling heavy workload in a **smart way**. On the other hand, since heavy workload has seasons which may be predictable, your answer will describe how you schedule time accordingly or to staff projects appropriately.

Another point in this question is how you handle pressure. Heavy workload always comes with stress. Even though your feeling is not stressed, you may become unhappy when processing lots of work. Typically, doing exercise or listening to music is a way to handle pressure.

Why were you fired?

When an interviewer is aware of your layoff, be **honest** about this fact. If your layoff was due to an economic recession or a business strategy change, your reason is usually acceptable. Besides giving the reason, what you did during the unemployment period is more of the interviewer's interest. Being fired was a negative event, but when you keep sharpening and augmenting your skills (e.g., taking training, creating a business, volunteering in a local community, etc.), the negative impact on you will disappear.

If you got fired due to poor performance, your reason does look bad. However, you may clarify the true underlying reasons, if any. For instance, the previous employer didn't invest in training; your previous boss was laid off as well because of his terrible leadership.

How does this position play a role in your career path?

Answer: Hunting for a new position is of course to get a paycheck, or a higher salary. However, the answer is not about money. Your answer can be given from various aspects. First, try to concentrate on your **motivation**. Further, a career path can have many variations, and the reasons why you choose a particular route are of importance. For example, if you want to go for a career in investment, why you choose a private equity firm rather than a mutual fund firm? Your answer has to provide good motivation.

In another aspect, your answer should cover your **career goals**. For people with years of work experiences, the motivation of their career paths was a past event, but the coming short-term and long-term goals are future events. Achieving the career goals is a driving force leading you to hunt for the new position.

What is your dream job?

Answer: Many candidates answer this question poorly. Bad answers are similar to the following: Make lots of money and retire; Minimize active work and gain a good amount of passive income; Zero commuting time; Flexible working hours; Employer provides free breakfasts, lunches and dinners; Free onsite daycare; Free parking. To be honest, these are features of my dream job as well. Unfortunately, bear in mind that any interview question wants to evaluate your fit with the position, rather than letting you chew the fat with the interviewer or asking your desired perks and benefits.

CHAPTER 3: JOB POSITIONS QUESTIONS

What made you choose our company?

Do your homework before coming to the interview? All your hard work would show in the information that you have gathered. Know what the current market stats say about the company and what recent new changes they have done.

Answer: This Company promises professional growth and compensations much more than its competitors. My research shows that the recent changes in its organizational structure will greatly benefit its workers and consumers. I will be more than pleased to be a part of this progressive company.

What salary are you expecting?

Do your homework before coming for the interview? You should be aware of the market trends for the particular job as well as how much that particular company is paying its staff. Considering that, you can come up with a range for yourself that best suits your experience and qualifications.

Answer: I have done some research on this and believe that the current rate is going somewhere between X and Z. I would be glad to start off working for you in the range for Y to Z as my experience adds some value to my application.

Have you worked in the same capacity before?

Most of the time people do not change lines and remain in the same field over years so if you have relevant experience then that is excellent to mention. Even if you have changed lines, try finding out how your past experience can help you carry out this job with ease.

Answer: 1-Yes, I have worked for three years in the same field for XYZ. My major responsibilities were xxxx.

What motivates you to fill this position?

This should bring out the best in you as a person. You are a perfectionist who wants to complete his job successfully and within time. You are motivated by the satisfaction of completing your job and helping out others excel in their line as well.

Answer: I am greatly motivated by the spirit of doing my job most diligently and be able to lend out a helping hand to others. I get a good night's sleep only when I am able to perform well at my job.

Can you put company's interest ahead of you?

The only answer to this question is yes. You cannot answer otherwise since it portrays a bad picture of you. Nobody wants to hire a person who gives them lower priority than others.

Answer: Yes, my company's priorities are most important to me than anything.

Why were you fired from the previous job?

You have to be honest but short. Nobody wants to hear about your sentiments but how you are dealing with this difficult situation and what you have to say. Anything said in a negative air would end any chances that you may have.

Answer: I became a victim of downsizing of which I am not sure why, but all I can say is, this gave me an opportunity to look for other better opportunities and here I am, looking at amazing new prospects that have the potential of professional growth.

If in future you want to discontinue working for us, what would be the reason?

This question needs special attention and would require excellent diplomatic skills. You will want to stay and not leave as your research on this company shows that it fulfills all your requirements. You are not planning to leave so do not say that you will leave for a better opportunity.

Answer: I do not believe that switching companies is necessary for professional growth. I believe in loyalty. I wish to excel in my field and gain experience by working for this company.

Are you looking somewhere else for job too?

The interviewer is trying to evaluate how much in demand you actually are. Your line of interest also shows in your selection of job positions and organizations that you share with your interviewer. Name a few good reputable companies where you had recently applied.

Answer: I have applied for the position of Quality Assurance Manager in XYZ, xxxx.

How long can you stay with us?

Committing to some timeline is not recommended. Your answer should be more diplomatic and rounded. You should be able to continue working for the company as long as it takes to help you learn and grow as a professional. You would want to work for the company and gain experience in your field. You would want to learn all about the organization and its functions so that you can add value to your contributions towards it.

Answer: I would love to work for XYZ and polish my professional experience by working with the masters of the trade working for this organization. I would find myself fortunate if I get to work for XYZ and would continue working for as long as my contributions can add something of value.

How will your education benefit you in this position?

Your education should be in accordance with the job to answer this one. Be prepared to answer with the best words relating your educational background with the new job's requirements. You should make the interviewer realize that your education will definitely benefit you in performing this job.

Answer: I have done ABC in xxxx, which is totally in accordance with this job's requirements. I am certain that I can carry out all the tasks and duties most efficiently because I was trained for this at college.

Would you change anything about your past?

You should come up with something, which could have helped you grow more professionally and you somehow missed or overlooked it. It could be a job offer, an opportunity to study further or anything. Your answer should ideally end in how you fixed the loss and have now improved your situation.

Answer: I got an opportunity to work with a great company a few years ago but I did not accept the offer because it required me to relocate. Now I have relocated twice and am willing to do it again if my job requires to as I have realized its importance in my field.

What was the biggest issue you had in your last position? What bothered you the most about your last job?

This is a good question so they know what common problems you might face in the workplace on an individual level. Interviewers will want to see what parts of a professional setting you might have been dissatisfied with. Many interviewees will be nervous, thinking that it's a trick question as what if you say something negative that this position actually includes! Don't be afraid, they just want to hear some brutal truths from you! Share how you truly felt in your last position but frame it in a way that you are able to also communicate something that is important to you in regard to work values.

Answer: In my last position, I felt like there was a lack of communication. Sometimes people would misinterpret what I said, and things weren't always expressed as soon as they should have been. I learned what good communication skills were from this position in the process at least.

How do you think you can bring about changes in this company?

You should answer by narrating examples of how your skills have helped you in the past and what valuable contribution you can make for this company. If you have done your homework properly you should know about the areas where this company needs growth and changes.

Answer: I believe with my experience and relevant skills; I can make excellent contributions for the progress of this organization. I know my hard work and passion towards my job would definitely benefit this company and help it grow even more.

Tell me what you know about this job role and its importance in the current market scene?

You should know the current market trends and needs for this job. You should be able to explain briefly using a few trends as an example so that your knowledge about this job is presented well in front of the interviewer.

Answer: ABC means xxxx. My research says that currently the market for ABC is xxxx.

How did you hear about the position?

Answer: This question offers a great opportunity to let you show your passion and **connection** with the company. If you have a reference (e.g., a friend, an alum, etc.) in the company, your answer should name the person and describe your good connection with the reference. If there is no contact in the company, it is fine to say that the position was found through a recruiting event, an article, or a job board. In either case, you should say you are excited about this opportunity, **and** what you can do for the company.

How much do you know about the position?

Answer: Answering this question is not very difficult. The answer can just cover what the **job descriptions** disclose. The answer should further detail the **skills** you can contribute to the job. If possible, create an action plan for the first 3-6 months after starting the job, and show the plan during the interview.

On the other hand, you **always** take this opportunity to ask the interviewer about the position in order to identify the duties that were not described in the job descriptions. Sometimes, a position is related to a specific project, which is highly confidential and cannot be disclosed in the job descriptions. In some occasions, a position is newly created, and you must rely on the hiring manager to explain the background of creating the position and his expected outcomes.

How much do you know about our company?

Answer: Before attending an interview, you always need to do research on the company. The company's **website** provides basic information and announcements. On the other hand, do your best to discover any **news** associated with the company. News articles usually unravel new strategies and new projects. Sometimes, analyses made by investment firms can also be used to help you discover in-and-out of the company.

Job descriptions may also reveal why a company is hiring a new employee. If the company is encompassing a new field, the job descriptions more or less show clues about a new strategic endeavor. However, if the opening is a replacement of a leaving employee, you probably cannot find special information about the company from the job descriptions.

Frequently, you can ask your interviewer a question related to the company, and his answer can reveal information about the company. Examples of such a question are: what do you like the most about the company? What is the strategic focus of the company? What is the culture? How many people in a team? How often a meeting takes place?

How can you apply your specific skills to help the organization (e.g., develop new products, generate revenues, achieve a sustainable growth, etc.)?

Answer: Answering this question is not very easy. First, you have to understand the position, and know the required skills fulfilling this position. Second, you need to know the benefits you can bring in to the company once your skills are applied. Examples of benefits include: better profits, higher yields, lower costs, higher revenues, innovative technologies, and new products. Ultimately, as long as the company generates better profits due to your direct or indirect contributions, your skills are valuable.

Are you willing to relocate?

Answer: Acceptable locations of a position are usually included in job descriptions. For example, a sales director in charge of the East Asian market can choose to live in Japan, South Korea, Hong Kong, or Singapore. Before your job application is submitted, you should have a sense where your job will be located. Sometimes, inability to relocate is a deal-breaker. In most jobs, you have to work in an office and the office location does matter. In some jobs, working places are not extremely important; for instance, business development managers and management consultants have to fly 4 days a week to visit clients, and their office locations do not make a significant difference.

How about your aspiration to do this job?

Answer: Answering this question is not easy. As we have stated, the interviewer has concerns. You may want to ask the interviewer to be more specific.

In general, the answer should express your motivation to work hard, and show you can quickly get onboard and learn the necessary skills. For instance, use the Scenario-Attack-Outcome approach to tell past experiences that demonstrate you are a quick learner.

Leveraging your past experiences to the new job is always a preferable answer. Even though you are switching to a new career path, previous projects must let you gain some unique experiences that can be extended to the new job. In addition, the underlying **attitudes** of identifying a problem, analyzing a project, searching a solution, and reporting an outcome should stay the same regardless of the fields. These attitudes should be emphasized in your answer.

Furthermore, if you have good **references**, you may request the interviewer to inquire more information from your references who can describe who you are, what you can do, and what you did frequently exceeds expectations. Since references are strong supporting evidence for you, passing the ball to references is a good strategy. Of course, you need to identify the best references before the interview; otherwise, you will screw up your job seeking process.

Another answer strategy is to lay out an actionable plan of commencing your new job. Sometimes, the hiring manager tells you the duties of the position (e.g., entering a new market or expanding to a new technical domain), and you can quickly respond him by enumerating possible execution steps to achieve the goals.

Why did you leave your last position?

Now this is the juicy part, where you start to reveal all the reasons that you are here. The employer is asking you this because they want to know why things didn't work out. Was the other position just not right for you? Did you leave your last job for a similar reason that you might end up leaving this job at this company you are trying to work at? They're going to want to know what happened to get a better insight into what went on. Spare them the dramatic details and keep it professional.

Answer: I left my last position because I felt as though there was no room for advancement. I lacked creative control and I felt that my voice wasn't being heard. I needed a positive change in my life because I want to continue to grow and move forward.

How did you find out about this current position?

The reason that employers might want to know this is because it will reveal even more about you. First, they are going to want to know if you know anyone that already works there. This gives them a personal recommendation which can be helpful in understanding who you are. They are also going to want to know if you were actively job-hunting and being proactive about finding a new position, or if this is just something that slipped into your lap. They are also going to be interested in figuring out if any of their marketing tactics to reach out to other potential candidates are working or not.

Answer: I actually found a listing for this job on an online job board. I have been looking and applying to several places and the objectives and job description of this position intrigued me.

What was the best part about your last position?

This is a question that will let your interviewer know what you value the most in the workplace. When you can discuss with them the benefits of a position, they will be more likely to see what things you are passionate about. Be honest with this, but of course keep it professional. You might have enjoyed that you had a few hours a day to sit on your phone after the boss went home, or maybe you liked that you got a free meal every shift. Keep it professional.

Answer: One of the best parts of my last job was the sense of community that was there. Everyone got along and we all managed to work together in a harmonious way, playing off each other's strengths and weaknesses. It was unfortunate when I had to leave, but luckily, I still keep in contact with many of the same people and have no issue including them in my life to this day.

Are you still looking for other jobs, and whom else are you interviewing with?

Interviewers might not always ask this question because it can be personal, but there are some that are legitimately curious to know where you are at in your current search. You might still be employed at your last company and only applying because you randomly spotted an ad for the job. If you also reveal that you have several interviews lined up, it can, in a sense, make you seem more valuable. However, don't lie, and leave it up to your discretion if you choose to share where you might be interviewing at.

Answer: I am still actively seeking out new jobs. I have a few interviews lined up the rest of the week that I am excited for. I'm grateful for any opportunity I have and am going to continue to do the best I can to try and find a position that works best for me and my life.

What will you require when it comes to training for this position?

This can be a tricky question, especially since you might not really know what the training process is about. They still might ask this because they want to get a better sense of the type of learner that you are. Will you be able to train quickly or are you someone that's going to require a little bit more time? Even if you know nothing about their training process and what employees have to do during training, you can still come up with a decent response.

Answer: When training, I will likely just require the materials needed to know what the tasks expected of me are, and how best to carry them out. It's also important to me that I have time to work hands-on, potentially lightly supervised for the first time, just so I can feel comfortable. I'm open to different learning environments and remember things rather quickly, so I'm not too worried I would struggle in training at all.

What kind of salary or compensation are you looking for?

They won't ask you what you've made in the past, and you won't want to ask them what you would be making without them bringing it up first. Still, if they ask you this question, then take that as your opportunity to be honest, and share how you truly feel. If it is your first interview, you might not want to talk exact numbers. Tell them whether you are looking for benefits or not, so they can at least share if this is something that they provide.

Answer: I'm looking to make the average, or slightly above the median salary for this position. I feel as though I have valuable skills that others way not, and my extensive educational background reflects the quality of work that I'll be able to bring to this position.

What about this position makes you want to work here? Why do you want to get hired?

The Why do you want to work here question is always going to be in the interview. It's not a trick question! Your interviewer will legitimately want to know why it is that you chose them. The obvious answer is, Because I need a job and I saw you were hiring. I want money. This is usually the first thing that we will consider when applying to a job. While this might be the truth, try to honestly remember why it is that you want this position and not another. Have your reason prepared before even making your way into the interview. When you can give substantial answers based directly on their mission statement, then that will give you a big advantage.

Answer: I want to work here because I have always been a lifelong supporter of this company. I have frequented the stores and I understand what the clientele is like. Not only do I think this will help me to be more passionate and dedicated to my work, but I think it helps because I will be more knowledgeable about what the business actually stands for. When I have this connection to the workplace, it is easier to go above and beyond because I have the confidence to know what my talents are and how the company will benefit from them.

What are you hoping to accomplish in this position?

This is a seemingly obvious question, but it can actually catch a lot of people off guard. It seems to be one of the most obvious questions that can actually reveal a deeper truth about someone who might be applying for the job. There are a few ways that you can answer this. You can discuss how you would like to move up to a higher position if that is something you believe to be an option. Alternatively, you can discuss how you hope to gain valuable skills if it is not a position that offers a lot of growth.

Answer: I hope while I'm working here, if hired, of course, that I can discover new skills that I may have and improve on things I need to work on while also helping the business thrive. I know the things that I need to improve on, and I have goals for myself. I think this company's goals and the goals I have for myself line up well together so that we can both mutually benefit from what I might experience here.

What traits do you think an employee in this specific position should have?

This is an important question because it will be specific to the employees and what you know about the company already. It shows them what you really think that you will be doing in the position if hired. The question is not just about you, it's about the position. You should put yourself in the perspective of the person conducting the interview, making it easier to see what they might be looking for. When you can do this, it becomes easier to know what a good answer would be. You might base this on a job description that you saw, or it could simply be something that you gathered as you discussed different things throughout the interview. Your response might be something like this:

Answer: I think that it's important for an employee in this position to be reliable. There are several people depending on them, and it seems as though there will be some high-pressure scenarios. If they can't be trusted professionally and personally, then that can put a wedge in the working environment.

Is it more important for people to like you in a managerial position, or for people to fear you?

This is a common question, especially if you are going to be interviewing for a managerial position. It's a frequent discussion of whether or not a manager is supposed to be feared or if they should be liked. Do you want to be the boss that's popular with everyone or is it more important that they become obedient and respect your authority? The best way to answer this is that you should be right in the middle of both.

Answer: I don't think it's a good thing to have someone fear you. If they are afraid of you, then they might not be willing to come to you with an issue, and they will be more scared to tell you what's on their mind. At the same time, it's not a popularity contest, so you do still have to be cautious of trying too hard to make everyone like you. Sometimes you have to be harder on certain people that need a little boost in their performance, so the authority in that situation is still important. The best leaders are those who fall right in the middle.

Let's say that after a few months with us, you discovered someone was doing something illegal. How would you go about this situation?

This is a question frequently asked, so don't assume that the business is already doing something shady just because they want to know how you'll react! They are just trying to catch you off-guard and see how you would react if you feel a little uncomfortable. What are your legal boundaries? How would you handle a potentially dangerous situation?

Answer: First, I would want to make sure that I have judged the situation correctly. Sometimes what seems wrong might just be misinterpreted, so I would wait for factual information and substantial evidence before making any real claims. Once I was certain that something illegal was happening, I would contact someone internally. Whether it's the supervisor of the department, or someone even higher up than that, I would go to them first to see what the best plan of action was. If seemingly everyone was involved in this, then from there I would seek legal advice or even contact the police if that was what the situation called for.

Would it be OK for me to call your current, or most recent, supervisors right at this moment?

Answer: They likely aren't going to actually do this when asking that question, but if they do, you should still be prepared. They want to see your reaction and are likely wondering if you've already told your references about this interview, or if that is something that you have yet to do. You should always make sure you've asked permission before using someone as a reference, so for this, your answer should be a simple, Yes!

What Would You Want from this Job?

If you've done your research, one of the easiest questions in any interview should be, What would you want from this job? The interviewer is checking to see if you want the type of job that is available. Your answer should be straight out of the job description.

Answer: In my current role, I'm the resident expert on the software programs that our firm uses to prepare tax returns. I enjoy leading training sessions for that software, and I'd like to do more of that.

CHAPTER 4: PROBLEM SOLVING QUESTIONS

How did you deal with a colleague you did not like?

This sort of question is used to judge the interviewee's potential as a team player and the ability to resolve conflicts. It also shows your diplomatic skills as well. Choosing the right words, you can easily answer this question making a good impression on the interviewer.

Answer: I have worked with a person whom I did not like very much as a person yet I appreciated him for his knowledge and superb logical skills. These attributes were not only helpful to him but were also very useful for the other colleagues. I started growing respect for him because of this and from then on we had a nice working relationship.

Do you work for money or job satisfaction?

Another tricky question. You cannot say that money is not important as it will trigger a whole new discussion, which you will want to avoid in any case. Job should be your first priority always. Try answering this more tactfully like the sample given below.

Answer: As they say money follows you if you work with passion, so I always go for job satisfaction. A job well done is my first priority but I will not say money is not important.

If this job does not fulfill your expectations, what will you do?

Will you leave us for something better? This question is to assess your loyalty and passion towards the job and the company. You have to prove that you will stay with reason so that it makes some sense to the interviewer.

Answer: I chose this job according to what I expect in terms of work, environment and work post. I believe that my expectations will be met and even if they do not entirely, I assure you that I am flexible enough to adapt easily.

What will you do if one of your colleagues is not actually doing his work properly and is cheating the boss?

This is not an open invitation to bad mouth your colleagues. Again this question judges how wisely you deal and answer this. You can show that you could be responsible as well as a good team player. You can narrate an incident if there is any.

Answer: I shall go to that colleague and tell him politely how his lack of attention to his work is affecting the overall quality of the entire team. I am sure this will help.

How do you handle a difficult situation?

Answering this question needs to be based on a Scenario-Attack-Outcome story describing the following: a difficult scenario, your method attacking the difficulty, and a good outcome resulted from your method.

Answer: Directing your answer to professional skills means that a difficulty happens due to your lack of experiences or lack of a minor technical skill. This kind of difficulty can be overcome by politely seeking advice from your mentor or supervisor, or by quickly learning the required skill. For example, an accountant is assigned to handle a tax report for a new international client, but he doesn't have an experience in international tax law. Therefore, he can overcome this difficulty by quickly exploring the past tax reports prepared by his colleagues and learning by himself the way of preparing the tax report for his new client. Alternatively, if learning by himself is not doable during a short time, he can request a help from a senior colleague.

When did you last fail in something? What did you do about it?

This is one of the most favorite questions to trap the interviewee. You should be prepared to answer this question. Try telling an incident when something did not go as planned and then what you learnt from it. Do not blame anybody. This will send negative vibes that can damage your impression on the interviewer.

Answer: When I was newly hired, I was assigned the role of xxxx. My performance did not satisfy my boss as he appreciated everyone else. I went to him and asked how could I raise the standard of my work and he let me know what went wrong with my performance. I learnt that I should discuss things more often with my boss before giving him the final version.

If you were the interviewer, how would you rate yourself on a scale of 1 to 10?

Rating badly shows lack of confidence in oneself and would diminish your chances of getting the job. Rating a 100% would mean you are unthinkably, incredibly awesome and you will raise unnecessary criticism against you. The best way is to remain somewhere between 8 and 9.

Answer: I would say a 9, as my professional qualifications and education are most relevant to this job. Furthermore, my work experience has groomed me in to a confident, capable and efficient hard worker but still I believe that nothing is perfect and that there is always a room for improvement.

How would you feel when your supervisor has less knowledge than you?

Expressing your open-mindedness is a direction to go. However, saying I am open-minded is not sufficient. The reasons behind the open-mindedness are more important.

Answer: First, you have to acknowledge that a leader must have ample knowledge than you in at least one field (either a professional skill or a soft skill). Because of this skill, you will respect him and his supervision. For example, a CEO may not know all the details of financing, legal, programming, product development, and marketing, but he is good at managing finance director, general counsel, software VP, and business development head. Therefore, you have to recognize the CEO's people management skill.

How did you react to a situation where a team member does not contribute his own weight?

Answering this question needs extra cautions. A safe answer is to say: **focus on your own assignment**. You do your best to get your job done, and further assist your supervisor to complete the whole project.

Answer: At work, this situation takes place likely due to that the team leader has bad management skills or that the teammate is a lazy person. These two reasons are hard to handle, and you have no authority to control your supervisor or teammate. As such, it is inappropriate to say: I will report to my supervisor or to my supervisor's boss or I will politely tell the teammate to work harder.

Can you sell me the chair that you are sitting on at the moment?

This is a question that might be specific to those who are interviewing for a sales position. Even if you won't be working with sales, numbers, or customers at all, it can still be a question that pops up. It is one that will show how well you can try and persuade someone. Are you a good schmoozer? Do you have a creative mindset that helps you to see the benefits even in something as mundane as a chair? They will ask questions like this especially if you are in sales, but the question might differ in how it is presented. They might say something like, Sell me this pencil, or ask you to sell another object that's around. Your sales pitch might look like this:

Answer: This chair is great for anyone who is looking to sit down. We all could use a break, and when we do decide to get that moment of rest, then this chair is going to be your top choice. It has a cushioned top that makes it comfortable for your bottom, especially for those sitting for long periods of time. It has features where you can adjust the height of the chair, so anyone can benefit from it. Not only does it have great comfort features, but it's aesthetically pleasing as well. Why don't you give it a try for yourself?

How did you react when your work was criticized?

Answer: This is an important question, and you need to give a Scenario-Attack-Outcome story. Remember to describe what your colleague or supervisor criticized about your work and how you adapted yourself to improve the work. Moreover, your answer should provide a viewpoint: Everyone can be my teacher, even though he is much younger than me. As long as a person has more experiences in an area than you, he can be your coach in the area. Thus, a criticism turns out to be a great asset for you.

How did you respond to a colleague who disagreed with your opinion or work?

There are two ways to answer this question. First, it's very possible that you never encountered this condition, and it is okay to say: I'm glad that this never happened to me. Second, if you had a similar experience, you can use the Scenario-Attack-Outcome approach to describe the condition, but the answer should emphasize the lesson you learned or show your good soft skills in turning the disagreement away.

Answer: When a co-worker or a supervisor put down your work, he may be correct or wrong. If he was correct, that means you must learn some lessons from this experience. If he was wrong, you need to describe how you changed his mind; however, in some cases, flipping the disagreement is extremely difficult because the colleague is in a higher rank than you, so your solution is to resort to your supervisor.

There is a possibility that the disagreement was just a different opinion rather than a judgment on your work, and it would be great if you can show how you negotiated with your colleague to reach a mutually agreeable opinion or persuade him to change his mind.

How did you do when you disagreed with a colleague?

The strategy of answering this question is to demonstrate your systematic analysis on your colleague's opinion or work, and to show your polite way of delivering the analysis to your colleague for changing his mind.

Answer: In a workplace, a persuasive way to disagree with an idea is to enumerate pros and cons of the idea. When there are more cons, the idea is unfavorable. There are many aspects to determine pros and cons. For example, in terms of technologies, you may consider scientific correctness, design complexity, implementation feasibility, and future maintenance. In terms of business, you may consider sales, marketing, financing, operations, fabrication, and information system. In terms of society, your evaluation may include political, economic and educational issues. Of course, some of these aspects may not be applied to your case, or your case can have additional aspects to consider.

How did you do when you disagreed with your supervisor?

When disagreeing with your supervisor, it is not enough to respond: I don't agree. You better express reasons for the disagreement. The reasons consist of your thinking or analysis, which leads to another opinion. Therefore, your disagreement should always come up with another suggestion.

Answer: After listening to your suggestion, your boss will accept or reject your proposal. If your suggestion is accepted, congratulations! Your proposal being accepted by the boss is the best story that you should tell in an interview session. Nevertheless, if your idea is rejected, that is fine because he is the boss! Unless your supervisor's idea is extremely unethical, you probably will stop here and respect his role as a supervisor.

How did you deal with nasty clients/customers?

Jobs in service industries, ranging from restaurant waiters and sales representatives to legal service professionals and health care providers, have to handle customers or clients daily. The service providers represent the images of their companies, which you should state in the beginning of your answer.

Further, your service philosophy should **be** unbiased to both good and bad clients. You always have polite attitudes and provide the best services to both types of clients. Sometimes, a good service can change a nasty client's mind.

Answer: In some cases, mitigating a client's complaints is necessary, because one less unhappy client can reduce any potential damage to the company. Since avoiding damages is your responsibility, your answer should describe how you spend extra efforts on the client. For example, a business development representative spends more hours on explaining his products; a realtor puts more efforts in explaining a home buying process; a customer service member issues a full refund to a complaining customer; a teacher schedules an additional meeting with complaining parents.

How do you manage your stress levels?

Stress is something that everyone feels. Even when we try our best to manage it, stress can still creep into our lives in seemingly small ways. The answer to this question is not about trying to deny that you get stressed. Instead, give a realistic method that you use in order to alleviate some of the symptoms. Here is a good answer:

Answer: I make sure that I am managing my time first and foremost. When I can prepare and prevent it helps to keep the stress from creeping up in the first place. I do know my limits, however, so when I am feeling stressed I will do my best to take a break so I can come back with a clear mind, better ready to focus.

How well do you handle criticism? Do you think criticism is important?

Criticism is important because it is what helps us improve. Some people will struggle to handle criticism and think that it means someone is personally attacking them. This can create a hostile work environment. For this question, you will want to make sure that the person conducting the interview is aware that you understand the importance of criticism and that you will be able to handle it if someone gives you a talk while on the job.

Answer: I can handle constructive criticism and take it with an open ear. It's not always easy to hear the things I might have done wrong, but I understand the importance of appreciating this so I can grow into a better version of myself. I also think it's critical that we find ways to have open communication within the office so that we can all feel comfortable improving each other as a team.

How do you prioritize your tasks?

Answer: I prioritize tasks first by how important they are. Then, I will number them and try to base what I'll do around this list. I also look to see if there are any tasks that I can quickly do to get out of the way. Sometimes it makes it easier to focus on the most important things if some of the smaller fluff is out of the way. I always ensure that I am focused on managing my time above all else.

What will you say if your work gets criticized?

You should be able to accept criticism with an open mind, as anything said against your work is to help you improve. Even if you do not like people criticizing, do not let it out. If you look at it positively, it gives you an opportunity to groom yourself as a professional.

Answer: I take criticism positively as it allows me improve myself on both professional and personal ends.

What steps do you take if someone you don't like in the office is really bothering you?

Answer: I would first make sure that I am showing patience to them. It is easier to be annoyed with things on bad days, maybe if I were stressed about something outside of work. I would do my best to be patient and not let the little things bother or distract me. If I had a close relationship with them and felt comfortable, I might say something, like 'Would you mind not chewing your gum so loudly?' If not, then I would avoid the situation, and maybe wear headphones if permitted.

Do you believe in taking risks?

The answer to this question depends on the job you are trying to get. If it involves taking risks then your answer should be according to that. In normal situations where risk taking is not encouraged, your answer should be that you are very cautious and avoid taking risky decisions.

Answer: I do not believe in taking unnecessary risks, but in some cases it becomes inevitable. Sometimes taking risks favors everybody, your company, you and others. A thorough analysis and careful planning can help taking risks a little less threatening.

When is the last time you lost something? Did you find it?

This is a question to show your level of responsibility. It's easy to say that we hold onto all sorts of responsibility, but at the same time, practical questions like this actually help to show what your level of accountability is. Try and think of what the last thing you actually lost was and find a way to relate it to this job.

Answer: The last thing that I lost were my house keys. I went to grab them and realized that they weren't in their usual spot. Then I retraced my steps and realized I had left them in the pocket of my pants, which was in the dryer! They weren't lost for more than a few minutes, but I was able to remember everything I did so I could easily find them.

CHAPTER 5: CLOSING QUESTIONS

When Can You Start?

If you prepare properly, there is a chance your interview could end with your being asked When can you start? Even if you don't get this question during the interview, you should prepare for it, since it will hopefully come shortly after the interview.

Answer this question truthfully. (Of course, you should answer every question truthfully, but for this question, candidates sometimes respond with what they think the interviewer wants to hear rather that what's realistic.) If you're required to give your current employer two weeks' notice, tell the interviewer that.

Also, it's okay to ask when the interviewer would like to fill the role. If they are flexible on the start date, you could negotiate with them. They might be agreeable to having you delay your start date so you can take some time off between jobs. However, they might also need someone to start as soon as possible. You won't know unless you ask, so I recommend you ask.

Answer. Do you have a specific date in mind when you want someone to start in this role? I'm required to give my current employer two weeks' notice, which I could do as soon as we negotiate the details of the offer. However, if you want someone to start later, I would be open to giving notice to my current employer, then taking a short period of time off before starting work with you. Let me know what works best for you.

This is a great answer because it shows a strong interest in the job, but it also shows that the candidate expects to negotiate a fair offer. You want to seem interested, but don't give the impression that you'll accept any offer. Given the opportunity, you should signal that you'll be interested in an offer, and you expect it to be a fair one.

Do you have any questions for me? (Is there anything you want to know more?)

At the end of every interview, they will always ask, Do you have any questions for me? Without a doubt, in some form or another, they are going to ask you this. Some people will think that this means the interview is over. They'll say something like, Nope! I think I got it all, thanks! This is the worst thing you can do!

When they ask this, the interview is not over. It's really the beginning of the second half of the interview. Never allow yourself to completely ignore this question. Always come up with at least one thing that you can ask. It shows that you are generally interested and that you want to become a part of the team, not just someone who wants the job to make money. Try to think of your own questions, but here are some good ones to ask in order to help you look professional and interested.

Near the end of an interview session, the interviewer typically gives you few minutes to let you ask questions. A lazy interviewer may open his entire session to your questions, without asking you any question. Regardless, the purposes of this question are two-fold: gauging your enthusiasm to the company and allowing you to better understand the position.

Basically, the questions you want to ask should be centered at the position, the projects, the company, and the career path. Alternatively, you want to ask the interviewer's perspectives on the **position** and the **company**. Below are some examples:

- What is the strength of the company?

- What is the strategic focus of the company?

- What are the competitors?

- What is the business model?

- What is the culture in the company?

- How many employees are in the division/company?

- Who are the clients?

- What is the difference between this position and another position XXX (e.g., finance manager vs. account manager; research scientist vs. programmer; team lead vs. director)?

- How projects are assigned?

- How do you staff a project?

- What is the workflow of a project?

- What are most important skills for this job?

- How many people in a team?

- How often do meetings take place?

- The supervisor of the position is promoted within the organization or from another company?

- What do you like the most about the company?

- What is the work style of the hiring manager (or the team)?

What Questions to Ask the Interviewer

What is the biggest challenge that other employees in the past have faced?

This is a good question that can help show the employers that you aren't afraid of what might be coming your way in the position. You've accepted that there are going to be challenges but that you are prepared for this! When you open yourself up and are willing to embrace challenges, then it makes you look like a more hard-working employee. It also gives you the opportunity to prove yourself. Whatever the issue is that they state previous employees have had, you can remind them that you are going to be able to overcome this uphill battle.

Is there anything we've discussed that makes you concerned I'm not the right fit for the job?

It can be challenging to keep track of everything you might have said throughout the interview. When you ask this, then you are covering all your bases. There might be something that you didn't explain well enough, stated in a way that they misunderstood, or there may be a topic that wasn't even covered in the interview. They will respond by telling you that maybe it's your lack of experience or something else on your resume that they saw. This will give you the chance to explain yourself further so that they have the truth when making their final decision.

What is the strongest quality needed for this position?

This question is for you as well. If you are interviewing for a desk position because you enjoy computer and paperwork, but they tell you that customer service is actually the biggest role in the job, then this will give you a warning to show that this job might not be the right fit for you. It will also give you another opportunity to prove yourself, giving you the chance to remind them why you are actually a perfect fit for the job because you already have that strong quality that they are looking for.

What is the most important responsibility that I will have?

This is similar to the question about what the important quality is. You will be able to get a sense of what the real job you will be working is. Those getting interviewed always focus on making themselves look as good as possible, but the person conducting the interview is going to do the same thing! They will want to make the position look good so that you might choose them if there are other prospective positions.

What is your history with the company?

You will want to know how long your interviewer has been there. If they say something like, Just a year, then this tells you a few things. One, it is a good sign that there is room for growth within the company and that they provide new opportunities. It also might be a sign, however, that there is a higher turnover rate and that some individuals might not enjoy working there for longer periods of time. If they say they've been there for a while, then you know it's a good place to work! It also helps to show your genuine interest in the company and the person that's asking you questions.

Why do you enjoy working for this company?

This is another question that lets the person conducting the interview know you are genuinely interested in this company. They might reveal some of the perks that you are wanting to ask about, such as an employee discount. You will be able to see the genuine quality of their response so that you can guess if they are really someone that likes the company or if it is just another job to them.

I noticed something as I was doing research on the company. Can you explain that to me further?

This is a great way to let the employer know that you were looking up the company and doing research before you came to the interview. When you can tell them that you were doing research, it lets them know that you are serious about this job and have a general interest in their company. It also shows that you are detail-oriented with a critical eye that can pick up on minor details hidden within their site. It can clear things up for you and also let them know that you are looking at the things that are shared about their company.

What is the team like here? What is the dynamic among employees?

This gives you a sense of the type of other employees that you might be working with. If you are looking for a working environment where you can make friends or one where you don't have to talk to anyone at all, then this will give you an answer about whether or not it aligns with the kinds of things you are hoping for.

Aside from what we've discussed, are there any tools you need from me, or any other research I can do in the meantime as the hiring process continues?

This is a final way to make sure that you are able to fully prepare for the next step. They will likely tell you what the next steps will be. They might say something like, I have four more interviews so I will let you know next week. This gives you the mindset needed to know if you should be nervous about what happened or be moving on and focusing on other jobs as well.

Anything Else

Sometimes, interviewers will conclude their questions with, is there anything else I should know about you? If they're still undecided about you, this is their way of seeing if you can make a compelling case that will sway things in your favor.

It's important that you focus on something positive for questions like this. Don't tell them that you have travel restrictions, you prefer to work certain hours, or you want a company expense account. Instead, use this question as your opportunity to tell the best story that you've prepared or to address unresolved issues from previous questions.

References

Some employers will ask to see your references. If you're interviewing for jobs, you should have three people who you've already asked to be references for you.

I recommend you bring a list of references to the interview. On that list, include the names of three references, their relationship to you, and their preferred form of communication. That way, the employer will know whether they should contact your references via e-mail, phone call, or written letter.

These references can be anyone who is familiar with your work. Ideally, you'll have at least one previous employer on that list. The other references could be teachers, clients, coworkers, or people from organizations where you've volunteered.

Avoid using family members and friends as references since they won't be considered impartial judges of your capabilities. You also don't need to include your current employer on your list of references. Since they may not know that you're looking for work, an interviewer will not expect you to list them as a reference.

Answer. Here is a list of three people who have agreed to be my references. The first is my previous employer who has since left the company where I currently work. She was my boss for over a year, so she's the best judge of my capabilities.

Next is the volunteer coordinator for the animal shelter where I volunteer. I help them with their bookkeeping, so he can also attest to my bookkeeping skills.

The third person on this list is my faculty advisor who worked with me when I was getting my accounting degree. She supervised me on several class projects, so she's familiar with my academic work.

I like this answer because it includes people who have a wide variety of experience with candidate. They can provide input related to work experience and academic capabilities. For your references, try to get people who have directly supervised you in a variety of experiences.

CHAPTER 6: QUESTIONS NOT TO DO

Do not ask questions that pressure the interviewer to tell why you shouldn't work for the company or what they don't like about the job. This will make them think they shouldn't offer you a job.

Do not ask about salary, benefits, or work hours. You can negotiate that once you have an offer.

This is a top concern for many employees. There is this sort of idea that you are supposed to want the job regardless of what the pay is when you are going through the interview process. While this would be true in the employer's perfect world, we have to face the fact that most of us wouldn't work at all if we didn't have to make money. However, you don't want to ask this during the interview because it will make it seem like the only thing you care about. They might bring it up, but wait until they offer you the job to discuss salary.

Do get them talking about why they like the company or why they think you would be a good fit for the role. Also, interviewers love giving advice. Don't we all? So, ask their advice for someone who might be joining their organization. That way, they'll be giving you advice as if you were their new employee. This has a powerful subliminal effect of transitioning their perspective from evaluating you to thinking of you as an incoming employee.

Don't!

Don't be modest: Interviews are not the place to be humble. You should proudly talk about your biggest accomplishments, your most relevant work experiences, and any major awards you have won. Interviewers like to hear about results and accomplishments, and they love meeting confident candidates.

Don't be personal: Don't talk about personal information such as family, friends, and hobbies that are unrelated to the job. Don't talk about religion, politics, your favorite sports teams, or any topics that could be polarizing.

Don't be negative: No matter how bad your previous jobs or bosses have been, don't say anything bad about them during an interview.

Don't be verbose: Don't go into too much detail in any specific area. As you practice your interview skills, find a brief way to answer each question so you're providing an amazing answer without repeating yourself or droning on with unnecessary details.

What You Won't Need to Answer

There are going to be a few questions that are unlikely to be asked and some which are actually illegal if someone were to ask them in this setting. If someone asks you any of these, in any way shape or form, you do not have to answer. If an interviewer does ask you this, they are likely unaware that they aren't supposed to be asking you. Some might still disregard legality and ask, but you should still do your best to change the conversation and not feel obligated to answer.

<u>Do you plan on starting a family? Are you expecting or trying to get pregnant? How many kids do you have?</u>

Any of these questions are not fair to ask you. An employer might want to know if you are planning on starting a family because they don't want to have to give out maternity leave. They might also question how many children you have so they can find out if you are readily available in the sense that you won't have to find a sitter for a last-minute shift, or that you won't prioritize kids over work. However, plenty of people have childcare in their life and other spouses or family members to help.

There are still always emergencies with children, so some employers might want to avoid this possibility by not hiring those with families. This is not fair to ask, so don't feel the need to answer! If your family life does matter, say you have a child that needs extra attention or if you are already pregnant, bring this up during the beginning stages of employment to ensure that they will not discriminate against you.

Do you have a boyfriend/ girlfriend/ husband/ wife?

Employers are not allowed to ask this. Most won't care, but it could give away your sexual orientation and lead them to discriminate depending on this. Just like the family question, you don't have to answer! If you want to talk about your partner, that's perfectly fine for you not to do so. Remember that you are not obligated to share this personal information with them.

What is the ethnicity of your family? What is your race?

If you have not disclosed your ethnicity, some employers might still be curious. They will know they can't blatantly ask, but they might ask about your family, asking if they are from a different country in order to determine your race. This is an illegal question that you do not have to answer. Discrimination based on race or ethnicity is illegal, and revealing this could cause the interviewer to be discriminatory based on who they are.

How old are you?

It is illegal for interviewers to ask what your age is. This is to protect against age discrimination. You don't have to answer this in any way. They might ask something like, How long have you been out of college? If you say four years, then they might assume you are still in your twenties. They might ask this in other cryptic ways. Don't answer! You can still share your answer if you want in ways that don't give away your age. You might say something like, I've had a few different opportunities to gain experience since college. This shows experience but not with a number attached. You can definitely share your age if you want, but if you don't feel comfortable doing this, no one is allowed to force you to share your age in the interview. If hired you'll have to fill out paperwork with your birth date, so it will eventually be revealed.

How much money do you make, or have you made in the past? How much debt do you have?

No one is allowed to discuss your pay with you. Just like the last question, look for sneaky ways that this is hidden, such as Do you think you were compensated fairly in your last position? they can discuss compensation with you about the current job that you are applying and interviewing for. They don't get to know your financial situation, including any outstanding debt, or the numerical amount of what you were paid in your last position.

What is your religion? Do you need time off for religious holidays?

This is illegal and could be discriminatory just like the question about race. Be aware of how they might phrase it by asking about holidays you celebrate. This is still not OK, and you don't have to answer. If they ask you about needing certain weekends off and time off here and there, that's OK, but it is not acceptable if the true intention is to just determine what religion you might be.

Have you been arrested?

They can ask if you have been convicted of a crime, but not arrested. It's better to be honest and open about your past, but you still don't have to share this information if you do not want to.

Do you use drugs/alcohol?

An employer will likely want to know if their employee does, especially if it's hard drugs. However, they are not allowed to blatantly ask. This could also be discriminatory for those interviewing that are recovering alcoholics or other recovering addicts, which is why you are protected legally from having to answer.

Change the Subject

Sometimes, you might run into an issue with an interviewer to the point where you don't want to continue with the conversation that you are having. Perhaps things took an awkward turn, or maybe you feel it getting to a point where the interview is ending but you haven't said all that you have to share. Whatever the reason is, it's important to have an idea of how you can turn the conversation around in your favor.

You also want to ensure that this is not just a stiff and overly professional interview. You are not there to just fill out a questionnaire. It should be an entire conversation. It's not a numbered list where you check things off as you go. It's a blend of topics that help to paint out exactly who you are so the person conducting the interview gets a sense of your character deep down.

In the right kind of conversation, you can actually become the leader of the conversation. So many people will wait for the person conducting the interview to say something, but you should never be afraid to take initiative and be the one to take the conversation to the next level.

There will be plenty of people that say all the right things, but you also don't want to get to a point where you forget to try and stand out. Many people will try to say what they think is the right thing that they are expected to recite in their interview. Don't do this. Stand out from the crowd and let your personality shine through. If you don't communicate your true personality, then you will just be based solely on other aspects, like your background, but this won't always be strong enough to land you the position. When they ask you an awkward question and you are not sure how to respond exactly, instead, ask them a question. It's important that you tell the truth in your answers, but at the same time, let them talk too. This will show that you are interested in the position and that you are good at answering questions as well.

Tell them that you also appreciate that they have asked the question. When they ask you something, don't just answer right away. Acknowledge what they said. It's funny you asked that because I have a story that relates, or That's a great question, I wasn't expecting that, are some phrases that could even help to buy you some time while you come up with the right things to say. Think of it like counting to 10 before you answer so that you can better ensure you aren't saying something that you don't mean.

When all else fails, tell a story. Don't talk their ear off, but sharing real, concrete examples will be better than rambling on with filler explanations that just paraphrases what was already said.

Tell them that you ... and guarantee that their understanding ...

CONCLUSION

Congratulations for reading this book. Ideally, you should capture the key concepts of the questions and develop your own answers. Then, you have to practice your answers multiples times.

Now that you are aware of all the things that you might be asked, it's time to practice!

Have others ask you these questions so you can give answers out loud. Rewrite some of the questions we asked in ways that the interviewer might ask if they were to change things up. Think of new answers, and remember the meaning and not just the order of the words that you want to say.

Remember that at the end of the day what matters most is that you stand out from the crowd. It's not easy to get an interview, let alone be the one they pick out of a large pool of qualified individuals. As long as you are authentically you, you'll have nothing to worry about.

You should highlight your experiences that are most relevant for that specific job. The employer isn't interested in your experiences that are unrelated to the position they are trying to fill. Those experiences might be important to you, but they're not important to the employer. Spend every minute of your precious interview time talking about experiences and skills that the employer will value in the role they have to fill.

Best wishes as you develop your own amazing interview answers.

CPSIA information can be obtained
at www.ICGtesting.com
Printed in the USA
BVHW011515030321
601595BV00001B/10